National Art Schools of Havana, Cuba

A TRAVEL PHOTO ART BOOK

LAINE CUNNINGHAM

National Art Schools of Havana, Cuba

A Travel Photo Art Book

Published by Sun Dogs Creations
Changing the World One Book at a Time
Print ISBN: 978-1-951389-17-8

Cover Image by Laine Cunningham
Cover Design by Angel Leya

Copyright © 2024 Laine Cunningham

All rights reserved. No part of this book may be reproduced in any form or by any means, electronic, mechanical, digital, photocopying or recording, except for the inclusion in a review, without permission in writing from the publisher.

The campus of Cuba's National Art School, currently known as the Instituto Superior de Arte, is one of the most important historical landmarks on the island. By rejecting the period's prevalent International Style, three architects created an entirely innovative form.

Catalan-vaulted brick walls topped with terracotta tiles enhance the organic feel. The use of local materials eliminated materials that embargoes made far too expensive to import. On campus, dance studios spread like shards of shattered glass around a central exterior space. The oval buildings and meandering walkways of the School of Plastic Arts evoke an African village. The Schools of Ballet, Music, and Dramatic Arts display similar groundbreaking concepts.

Political and economic issues prevented the school from being fully completed. It is still open today, offering tuition-free higher arts education to Cuban nationals. The site is an official National Monument as well as a 2003 UNESCO World Heritage Tentative List site.

BREEZEWAY

WINDWARD

CRUCIFORM

CLASSICAL

CATAN

WELLSPRING

GANGWAY

GALLANT

WALNUT

GRAFT

OPTICS

SCULPTURE

THUMP

WINDS

INFLECTION

LEEWARD

OPENING

VISAGE

BROW

FATHER

IF ONLY

MOTHER

CHORUS

STAGE

YURT

TRANSIT

GALLOP

QUAD

READY

SLIDE

STANDOFF

ALLOW

RHYTHM

HOVEL

BIRTHING

TITLES IN THIS SERIES

Havana, Cuba
Old Havana, Cuba
The Malecón, Havana, Cuba
Central Havana, Cuba
Vedado, Havana, Cuba
Regla, Havana, Cuba
Miramar, Havana, Cuba
Streets of Havana, Cuba
Classic Cars of Cuba
Classic Cars of Old Havana, Cuba
Classic Cars of Havana, Cuba
Spanish Colonial Havana, Cuba
Gardens of Havana, Cuba
Verge Gardens of Havana, Cuba
Cats of Havana, Cuba
Colón Cemetery, Cuba
National Art Schools of Havana, Cuba

www.ingramcontent.com/pod-product-compliance
Lightning Source LLC
Chambersburg PA
CBHW040002080526
44586CB00027B/2860